Girl on a White Porch

A Breakthrough Book
No. 51

Girl on a White Porch

Poems by
Nancy Schoenberger

University of Missouri Press
Columbia, 1987

Copyright ©1987 by Nancy Schoenberger
University of Missouri Press, Columbia, Missouri 65211
Printed and bound in the United States of America

Library of Congress Cataloging-in-Publication Data
Schoenberger, Nancy.

Girl on a white porch.

(A Breakthrough book; no. 51)

I. Title. II. Series.
PS3569.C5237G5 1987 811'.54 86-16130
ISBN 0-8262-0620-4 (Alk. paper)

∞™ This paper meets the minimum requirements of the
American National Standard for Permanence of Paper for
Printed Library Materials, Z39.48, 1984.

This book was brought to publication with the assistance
of a grant from the National Endowment for the Arts.

For Tom Schoenberger, 1954–1973

Acknowledgments

The author gratefully acknowledges the following journals and books in which several of these poems originally appeared:

The American Poetry Review: "Epithalamion," "Stars, Fish," "God's Sun," "In Street Light"

The Antioch Review: "Galleria," parts 1, 3, and 4

Antaeus: "From the Glass House" (published here as "The Taxidermist's Daughter"), "Audubon's Shrews"

Columbia: A Magazine of Poetry and Prose: "'Easy the Life of the Mouth,'" "On Frida Kahlo, a Deer Passing into the Forest," "On Frida Kahlo, Turning Away from the Children"

Cutbank: "Cypresses," "Girl on a White Porch," "Flambeaux," "By Certain Rivers"

Where We Are: The Montana Poets Anthology (Smokeroot Press): "The Beast's Palace"

Ploughshares: "Quiet and Getting Quieter"

Poetry: "Train to Seattle, Christmas Morning," "A Small Thing"

The Sonora Review: "Sleeping Mother," "Perdita"

The Southern Review: "This Is Missoula," "After Camille," "In This City," "Shiraz," "October Poem: Baynard's Irises"

The Taxidermist's Daughter (Calliopea Press, 1979, distributed by Graywolf Press): "After Camille," "The Taxidermist's Daughter," "This Is Missoula," "The Beast's Palace," "Azalea"

With special thanks to the National Endowment for the Arts, to the Rockefeller Foundation's Study and Conference Center in Bellagio, Italy, and to the Writer's Residency at Centrum, Port Townsend, for their grant and residencies, which enormously aided in the completion of this manuscript.

N.J.S.
New York City
September 1, 1986

I

II

III

IV

The Devins Award for Poetry

Girl on a White Porch is the 1987 winner of The Devins Award for Poetry, an annual award originally made possible by the generosity of Dr. and Mrs. Edward A. Devins of Kansas City, Missouri. Dr. Devins was President of the Kansas City Jewish Community Center and a patron of the Center's American Poets Series. Upon the death of Dr. Devins in 1974, his son, Dr. George Devins, acted to continue the Award.

Nomination for the Award is made by the University of Missouri Press from those poetry manuscripts selected by the Press for publication in a given year. George Garrett was the judge for all poetry selections made in the Press's Breakthrough Series for 1986 and 1987.

I

My Grandmother's Quilt

It's not so much the "garment of contentment"
she pieced for herself, but an old quilt
that tells the world's story in random fabrics:
here's Noah's ark, aloft on a cotton flood,

the two by two of cambric animals
snipped from the stained tablecloth
and made part of the story. The creweled borders?
Blue waves of the deluge, God's wrath.

Let the dominant yellow patches stand for Ruth
in the alien corn, for blonde fields
where we stood, homesick and drowning,
in every state of the Union. Here's Egypt,

these chains of stitches where slaves wept
over the shaved heads of their women.
Now we come to Caesar's things: coins, medallions—
pieces of silk from mother's party dresses.

Scattered throughout are white cotton triangles,
butterflies, really—the resurrection
and the New World—pristine, innocent,
a little something for contentment.

The whole thing is moth-eaten (hordes
of locusts), leaving gaps in the tale,
primal O's where the wind blows through
and the threads of the story are lost, broken . . .

not a memento but a history in miniature
from my verse-quoting grandmother,
whose own girlhood stories
were buried with her.

Cypresses

Pulled by the roots from a hot Southern town
where we unfolded like geraniums, grafted
to the icy bayside of Northern wilderness—
fast cars, fast girls, fast tongues!—
we fasted till your asthma kicked up, the frigid air
sliced through the bellows of your lungs.
At knife point once you gave up your allowance.
I dyed my hair and applied lipstick with a vengeance
and let the boys come, I didn't care.
You were summer's own fair-haired boy.
You would rather be funny than smart. All night
at your blonde violin, playing the same tune over again,
getting it right, the ode to joy you understood
at fourteen and finally got right, all of us
yelling at you to *shut up*. At seventeen you went under,
went into the trees in your new Triumph. I've gone
back South once or twice, though you never will.
The last time I sat at Cafe du Monde
I watched the pigeons swirl like a cape
around Jackson's horse, in Jackson's square,
sky gilded like a rococo sky, a place
like any other place, to tell the truth—
perhaps more pink. I went to Pierre Part
and the labyrinthine channels of water,
now empty of significance. Near Audubon
where the silted river slides to the sea
with its cargo of Northern sorrows, I saw cypresses
hanging their hair in park's charred light.
Now you come to me in dreams and tell me *it's too cold*
though the long roots of the trees wrap you round
and winds still blow warm from the Gulf.

Perdita

"Your girlhood was finished, your sorrows were robing
you with the readiness of woman." —Derek Walcott

Adrift in New Orleans in a yellow dress
in yellow October, between jobs, boyfriends,
friends, and schools, in the first, fresh

heat of denial, slipping between the deepened
shadows of the live oaks on St. Charles
toward the Audubon Park seal pool, whose deep end

is shrouded, past the stone halls
with their museum of fishes: garfish
and shoepick, and the lawless

and terrible snakehouse (languish-
ing anaconda, limp coils of snakeflesh)—
like a spoon rattling a dish

she strode through the brilliant mesh
of shadows on Greek-copied statues, the rays
of spiders' threads dress-

ing the larger web of trees, and the spray
off the seals' impossibly sleek backs
(oblivious, uncle-faced!);

laughed at the seals and the fact
she could go in any direction, could whirl
across the miniature tracks

of the toy railroad she rode as a girl
through the lugubrious oaks of Audubon.
Who would have said, in that new world,

she would go home and, thoroughly undone,
cut off her hair like Jeanne D'Arc,
but without the angels? It had begun:

she left the park
and its paradise of statues,
threw out her summer dresses, locked

in some weird penance. But sometimes it rose,
it opened like a gate left ajar
for a whole morning. Lies?

Fictions? Something stirs,
as when Giulietta Masina in the old film
is hypnotized by a traveling huckster:

the swilling paesanos are hushed, the realm
of the theater changes: Look! She's a girl of sixteen.
She dances, and in her arms

are her first flowers. On winter evenings,
Perdita, just think of it. Go back to the park.
The spell is broken, but the statues are living.

Girl on a White Porch

Where do they go, the young boys, glass
splintering their hearts? Called back?
It was the same river: car overturned,
his yellow hair covered the rocks like grass.
Somebody held him, he would not get up.
Who was that girl who held her brother,
her blue dress and the evening finished?

In those days the shell road followed the river.
Alone on the porch swing, among the wisteria:
the girl and her brother.
And the trees heavy with oranges,
and the heat on their limbs like a hand
through the hosannas of the tree frogs.

Rain settles on the elm. A Keatsian mood
contaminates the lawn, tells the tale
of their innocence, the wet streets
shining like licorice. Because in poems
we weep for ourselves, in sepia weather
that spreads like a river.

When we are through with nostalgia,
will the two halves, memory and desire,
finally call them back?
No more a summer of hothouse flowers,
girl on a white porch and all the wisteria
falling to touch her.

Traveling with Mother

We were nowhere. The road unrolled
through yellow hills. Mother drove
her Plymouth Fury swathed in silence,
her skirt bunched up around her suntanned legs.
Dusk formed its cumulus over the earth.

We passed a grove of birches—speechless
trees, their limbs like women's limbs.
Like the dead who speak to us in dreams
they wait patiently, and in my cruelty
I will not free them.

Turned inside out, the landscape
hurtled by while we stood still.
I saw it shivering and turning back—
cows huddled in drifting fields,
the parting glances of the birches.
We drove straight through that landscape
without speaking.

Audubon's Shrews

Among the watercress Audubon's shrews
upturn a worm, pink as their noses.
They're not cuddly, but we can imagine the world
they inhabit: the earth moist, edible, ingenious-
ly laid out with its underground caverns,
its delicious humus.

                      A nearby farmhouse
the color of summer looms from a light mist.
Children's shrieks hang in the wind like gliders
over the willows and the birches are perfect.
A man plows his field, tiny as Icarus. His horse
arches her pretty neck. Whose is this,
this stillness, this place of shared concerns?
Something drifts from its hermit's nest, a beast
in a dream of flight. Below, the slow
shrews, some sparrows, a crow with a black
shoe. One will swoop, one will cry out.

In Street Light

—for Susan

Even now, under a dull sky, this road
dims and fools us. Left or right?
By the pond's rim, or those smooth trees,
the whispering crape myrtles? The birds
have gone home and Venus brightens,
caught in the flat lake.

Our bikes flash in street light—
we spin through the dark, each breath,
each space to the next stalk,
such easy flight. We glide like skiffs.

Across the lake, factories light up:
pure yellow fire, blackened stacks and shouts.
When the barn burned down we heard the cows
for seven miles. We were just girls. Black figures
move along the lawns, bringing in the chaises,
turning off a hose. We are the only ones alive

and it's been years.
I can still see you, your white arms,
the owls just beginning.

Azalea

There were no words for it,
the arm's strength and the tender
glance. The river beat
its crooked path through both of us,
the wind saying its name
over and over: speak, speak.

She went away. Flowers
took back their tongues.
This is not my mother. We're fooled. Father
eats and sleeps, sleeps and eats.
Now her bright scissors hang from her apron.
She wants my hair.

And in the long days under the porch
by the peeling birches, I formed my code:
it's these mountains, hunched and bitten
by winter, these rivers
where fish sleep
and men have quietly cut
dark holes in the ice.

The snow is piling up.
Horses starve in their pastures.
Somewhere azaleas burn on, as when
she held me on the chaise lounge,
the moon released from its rushes
by the white lap of the lake,
the nothing we could name
like ashes, like cold sleep,
from which we will not wake.

After Camille

These streets are gray as shale, as a heron's wing.
The loud wind rules the trees. Times like this
I go back to her dark house, that wormwood bump
on the river's careless lip, orange trees so thick
you never knew just what the house looked like.

Through the old rooms that held her fans,
Nana's mirrors and fine bowls, the pictures
of father, came the long pulls
of the barges and tankers. How the weather
soaked your skin, like a girl's raggy doll
thrown in a tin tub!

You'd think sun would break through
that cloud like a pearl's shell.
At dusk odors rose, the wind rolled
in tar and machine oil. You could smell
fish, the gulls' leavings, and the damp
mimosa. Here's where father was little.
Mother pulled water from the sulking well.

Now they're gone. I'd swear
the lapping of the river where we fished
hungered for the house's root. The grownups talked
in the kitchen's yellow light: sell or plant? *Oranges
in the flood.* We'll float this house to New Orleans
and sell ourselves. The river rises. Barges
bear gold down the Mississippi. I once rode

my father's sloping shoulders. They say catfish
comb those rooms where we once slept. Launched,
I come to waterways to drink the dark. Those
trees just bend, the rain says *I win.*
What remains the river doesn't want.

The Taxidermist's Daughter

Always long afternoon shadows
began leaking from tame leaves
near the plot of sunflowers, the valuable
statuary, chickens restless
as the best game cocks paired off
and started their dance,
father his work

restoring the draggled animals
that had gathered all morning
in the pine loft above the house,
from the wild Atchafalaya,
and Arkansas turkeys,
their Indian headdresses
limp and smeared and asking
for new life. The squirrel
that one day would fly again

in the showcase, and again
in my dreams, in dream-walks
through the glass house, fly
next to the lynx
and the rare white fox.

And the tamed dogs eyeing their masters,
and the fighting wild rooster,
my sunflower drifting over the gravel
marking the day's path. I wanted to help:

carry blood in a bucket,
order the glass eyes
from the warehouse of missing parts.
I wanted to help in your dark,
private work in the loft.

Nights the gray squirrel rattles the roof,

rubs the glass where his stuffed mate
swoons in the final leap. I can still see you
bent over your work, shucking and stitching,
fur stuck to your apron. Choose me,
father. All these years I wanted to say
choose me, as you bent down
to put the last touch
to the beautiful wood duck.

My Mother's Dresses

When we were girls we watched our mother dress
on humid nights, her slips and stockings hung
from bureau drawers. Her party dresses shone
on their hangers, scattered about her room—
my dresses now. The emptiness of dresses
strewn on beds, holding their form, a form
shaped like a face: the breasts as eyes,
the skirt hiding a mouth. (I see her shorn
hair, her teardrop earrings like tiny chandeliers.)
And all the outgrown dresses of my girlhood
on summer days—homemade, tiered,
festooned with eyelet lace—those dresses
hang as though they always knew us.

II

Flambeaux

"Sing your songs, Rupert the Rine,
but I'll not listen, though they tell me
you've a sweet voice." –Jean Rhys, *Wide Sargasso Sea*

Because the woman was in paradise first,
the paradise of her body: a hybrid, Creole gift
of white skin, eyes dark as a marmoset's,
and the paradise of frangipani, even of humidity
which bathes the thing and washes it,
and slows the passing of time, like a clock
thrown in a river, winding down . . . her auntie's
cotton stockings, cotton drawers, cotton slips,
all washed fresh and ironed on a hot day
when the work girls come laughing home from church.
The first thing that burns is the sun doused in the ocean,
and the same burning in Our Lady of Immaculate Conception,
framed in the parlor over the armoire
(her heart with its sword on fire),
and the burning of the boys' flambeaux
at carnival, because the black boys carry their flames
out of the heart of the island, on all of the islands.

Because the woman was in paradise first
there was no where else she could go
but down, over under, through and into,
the sound of carnival carried into the trees,
the wild, frangible girls in their feathers and gold,
and like the cypresses that drink up the sound of the river
she drinks up the sounds of the carnival, though her auntie
puts cotton in her ears and into her own ears . . .
Now they have lit their torches and begun their dances
and the woman, watching from her safe veranda,
is infected with those flames

just as her mother's house married the fire
as she would one day marry the fire
rushing headlong into the caesura
burning up her days in a cold place in a red dress,
the only thing that burns and consumes
in her purgatory of snow, in distant England.
Sing your songs, Rupert the Rine,
all these islands is burning now.

On Frida Kahlo,
Turning Away from the Children

The sun, as always, illuminates
what is: *wells hills trees*, the trees
in their column of sound
swaying from yes to yes
in their long patience.
Soon it is evening. The children
will sing in the streets,
a spoonful of ink pouring into the sky,
bleeding and draining and faithful to itself.
Their little voices a net to catch the night,
a net going back through generations of childhood,
dolls in their buckled shoes,
soldiers and confirmation dresses.
She is caught in the net with its thousand hooks.
Tired of this body which persists
in its ignorance,
its braces and wires,
its Lucullian dresses,
she is pulled and rocked.
Though she turns and turns
her face to the wall,
incarnadine, she cannot
get out, and the children
make with their songs the sounds
of her wounds: their little songs,
their little sparrow songs.

On Frida Kahlo,
a Deer Passing into the Forest

As if the trees had hands.
She is beautiful in her little clearing,
a deer with a woman's face. Troubled
as St. Sebastian, her flesh quivers
with its armory of arrows.
Where do we lie down, one on one,
to make the world, half-animal,
half-human? She has a mammal sorrow
and it takes her, deer-swift, into a dark
wood dark as her dark hair. A melody of color
trills from her hooves. Her sister wind
(the trees in their magnitude)
also abideth, darkened and chilled.

"Easy the Life of the Mouth"

When Yvonne saw her vision of the Christ
enter her bedroom her mouth in astonishment
opened and her arms went up, palms out,
to ward off his glowing presence. Silence
emptied from her mouth into the dark halls
of the convent-hospital, the silence
of astonishment, among God's brides.
Among God's brides she was the chosen one.
Later, back in school and fairly normal,
she wrote a poem about the bridegroom who
waits to draw her soul out through her
mouth, her promiscuous mouth,
as if the soul were a swallowed fish
or the mouth a cave where darkness collects.
Now she carefully keeps
her mouth shut on its wafer of silence
when entering a church or cemetery–
wherever one expects a ghostly presence.
The rest of us laugh and eat,
scream our delight, examine our teeth
in mirrors, allow our mouths to be entered
by different things–let the world
pass through us through our mouths!
Which is why the gods love song
for the mouth is open and the breath
which animates the world moves out, a chord,
a silver rope of sound that binds up souls,
like smoke leaving the burning houses
and pouring out. Easy the life of the mouth.

A Beautiful Chill
Runs Through Every- and Nothing

So the fabled girl in her stone villa

under a spell (a bargain
struck between desire and nature) has a kind of will.
She allows the statue to move her, its arcane

machinery set in motion. The villa
is hushed, sumptuous, locked in its circle
of glaciers, a glazed lake, a beautiful chill

which polishes all surfaces: ecru walls, gilded
mirrors, doorknobs, and gleaming tubs.
Outside her terraced and tapestried cell, the melted

snow forms little peaks and valleys, a sub-
lunary miniature of the stone-faced mountains, mimicking
their crags and hollows, their rubbed

shoulders: gnomish Alps, diminutive Himalayas. The icing
drips, the icy lights come on.
A beautiful chill runs through every- and nothing.

He never actually appears, unless as beast—nonhuman—
or a flutter of wings. In Cocteau's version
he's a magnificent bridegroom, a Byronic lion,

or else he's known by his mansion
which can never be made visible to others.
Poor Psyche pours his wine, it's river water. The handsome

porticoes are common poplars.
His riches can't be shared or admired,
therefore they are nothing. So her sisters

go away pitying, satisfied at last,
leaving her with her armful of calla
lilies, which are really straw–or are they? Vast

tracts of snow cover the mountains, snow falls
on lake and garden.

Sleeping Mother

Now, where the mad are assembled and bound
each in her own corridor of bliss,
I walk among them with my gloved hand, all grace
and polish. I pace, I stoop to kiss
this one's milky shoulder, to smooth the rat's nest
of another's hair. They turn and hiss.
The light I think is the color of milk, viscous;
the old, ruined light of the Masters, of women
with shaved heads in peeling corridors.

In another part of the forest I followed my mother
into her cottage. I watched as she got into bed and slept.
I watched as a yearling deer entered her bedroom.
I watched as he lifted his hooves from the flagstones
and reared over Sleeping Mother. I watched as he
placed his mouth on her mouth. I felt the weight
of his hooves on my shoulders. Sleeping Mother,
how can I help when they finally come,
when they shave your head and send you, weeping,
back to your own silent country?

In This City

In this city, the dead still walk among us.
Poor Richie, gone nine years, stands on that corner.
He sees, he passes by without a flicker.
I'll find my brother Tom, blond still and scarred,
asleep at noon on somebody's trimmed lawn.
What do they eat? Where do they find clothing?
What draws them, empty-handed, from the rivers?

I think they love the slanted light of winter,
earth's dangerous tilt. It lets them in.
They don't need to be remembered.
The stars still look the same from this small planet,
bold Orion and the seven sisters!
The avenues still blaze with the world's business.

Don't even speak–your tenderness might hurt them.
They come for the weather. All their sorrows now
have gone past healing, something a restless wind
spreads over the country.

Quiet and Getting Quieter

Start in a farmer's field, his daughter gone
forever this time, snow dusting
the corn stalks, the abandoned Chieftain,
coyote fur on the cattleguard. He hears
what's not there, and the usual noises.

Go underwater. The sea grabs the diver
and breathes for him. He hears
heartbeat, he hears the current
dragging her sad chain.

Consider the puffin
gorgeous in spring snow.
In the attic of childish desires
puffin is king–sentimental,
avuncular.

Now the farmer returns to his birches,
their leaves like tiny smiles.
A woman hitched to a dogsled,
long-legged, bleeding, slips through
the white woods.

October Poem: Baynard's Irises

If we are waiting for the invisible to gather
and step forward like the recalcitrant
prince he is, we are disappointed.
Study instead the Baynard irises,
flocking and leaning like geese in motley.
The vase restrains them, reeling them in
with its cobalt and tombstone hues.
Is that a cobra or a dancing woman
asway on its glazed surface? Her cloak spreads
like a final gesture, a mourner
creeping downward through winter
on spiral stairs. She must be beautiful,
she must be ruthless, as the room leans
toward her: the ivy drifts,
lucent and patient. Books lean as well
at a dangerous angle–*Jane Eyre*, *Galileo*.
Did I mention her spine enameled in scarlet
and the spot, the widow's hourglass?
Even the pumpkin has turned to face her–
its features inchoate, its blind head
ripe from its lumpen birth. That patterned
wing chair, jailed in the sun's stripes,
holds its arms open. She suffers them.
Arabesques on the couch line up in chorus.
Peonies huddle on the sleeping carpet,
prized of the thousand things.
And the cut-glass decanters are rigid
with purpose–all soldiers
to her Carmen. All follow her
down, down, down. To her dark home.

God's Sun

Winter again. Always the sky in earnest
with its rich skirts, its clouds of organza
rushing headlong to Madagascar. God's sun
shines on the female world.
God's sun quiets the shrieking winds.
Look! You can believe this! Put up your peaches,
shelve the asparagus for next August.

But the door closes
year after year on somebody sleeping.
She sleeps so she will not work.
She sleeps so she will not eat.
In the zero hour, ice ticks its clock,
the softwood floor groans and snaps,
frost hardens in the glass. Who will wake her?
Who will love her enough? Not the sun,
with his busy hands of fire. Not the winds,
with their secret language of blame.

The Beast's Palace

Always beside the bedstead
on the porcelain table, the red rose
which was my undoing. He never comes
though nights I hear his step
and as though a breath stirred, the curtain
is lifted: I can see moonlight
washing pebbles where goldfish circle
in the still dark of the vault.

He is somewhere in this house.

So the moon beginning to wash thin,
to turn back her face,
I began my search. The candle sighed
and wept; the shadows it threw down
were at first like small birds
suddenly giving up flight

and in the dark
this fine house was a ship
on a mountain peak, a stranded
and hollow ark. The door opened

where the beast lay sleeping.

O my friend, how could I know
you walked with a crippled step, horned,
hooved, and speechless? Our eyes met–
had you meant to speak? But those afternoons,

the sun's stripe
laid across the bushes, and then
your steps on the pebbled walk

as you came each night to forgive me
my disguises. We are awake
but the spell, the spell–

it is just beginning.

III

GALLERIA

1. *"Virgin with the Child and the Angel"*

–Fra Filippo Lippi, in the Gallery of the first foundling hospital

Cruelty runs through them like a whisper:
these images are hard won and we'll suffer for them.
Did the stricken foundlings live here with these paintings?
Were they comforted by angels? This angel looks right at
    you,
a child himself, a clear-browed boy. How our versions
of beauty differ, yet they are beautiful, Filippo's novice
whom he later ran off with. Botticelli would carry
those clear-browed youths, that beauty of line
into his own work. Was he captured by his master's mistress?
His Venus resembles her, his Madonnas and Goddesses.
Filippo's Madonna contemplates Nature. The child instructs
    her
supported by his angel, their skin like touched gardenias.
They are contained in a series of circles.
Will the boy cast off his angel's dress and run shouting
into the market? We're glad Filippo and his nun will sin,
among the thousands who vowed and sinned, embraced
the flesh that tortured with its genius, beauty a form of
    genius.

2. "The Annunciation"

–Beato Angelico

Surely all you want to know of angels
is in this painting. He or she is not so much beautiful
as graceful, full of grace, her fanciful
bird's wings every hue of the spectrum.
She is contained in a series of half-circles,
the half-circles of the loggia. The black band
that vibrates and allows the spirit to enter: Mary
bows her head so as not to disturb it. Another curiosity:
the brown picket fence with pointed slats, a modern fence.
Have fences changed so little in five centuries?
(It looks like the fence around my father's house.)
The trees and the grass don't change, they are innocent.
In the cool morning, she is alone when the angel comes.
They bow, they cross their arms, they mirror each other.
Something about the coolness of the woods,
the coolness of architecture.

3. "Creation of Man"
—Bartole di Fredi

Christ is alive with fiery wings
or so it seems; it's God the Father.
Behind Him crouch diaphanous winged
spirits, entities. They are like his own
elaborate wings and they suspend him.
Naked Adam lies slumbering, his feet
touching God's, forming the point of a triangle
whose third side is a beam from God's eye.
It looks like the man's spirit is entering his body.
The trees, the beautiful trees, are sexual,
particular. God's angels have bat wings
and why not? Adam's penis is long
and pale and lies against his thigh.
My guide and I sigh, eyeing this
fresco.

Naked Adam, touching God's particular
elaborate wings and they suspend him.
I sigh. Pale and lies against his thigh.
Eyeing this: spirits, entities.
They are like his own. The man's
spirit is entering his body. Fiery wings.
Whose third side is a beam from God's eye.
God's eye: behind Him crouch diaphanous
winged spirits. The beautiful trees, the
sexual fresco. Or so it seems. Christ is alive
and why not? Bat wings. Adam's penis.
Forming the point of a triangle, my
guide and I eye this, slumbering
spirits.

God's angels have bat wings.
Diaphanous fresco: slumbering

Adam, his feet touching God's.
And why not? Is long and pale and lies.
Christ is alive with fiery wings
whose third side is a beam,
the man's spirit. They suspend him.
Eyeing this, I sigh. My guide
is alive or so it seems; behind Him
crouch spirits, entities, the beautiful
trees. Adam's penis is like his own.
Elaborate, touching God's. Naked
Adam, from God's eye, forming the point
of a triangle. Man's spirit
is entering his body, particular,
sexual.

4. "St. Gregory Appears to St. Fina and Announces Her Death"

He appears like an icon hovering in space,
a Byzantine, teardrop jewel
suspended by six *putti rosa*.
One imagines they turn like a wheel
and the vision moves through space
by this circular motion.

St. Fina and her maidens regard this
with proper astonishment, their hands raised,
supplicant. The light on her wall is decanted–
aged, layered, stained with the sediment
of centuries, like light moving across the cement
floor of an old hotel pool.

From the doorway you glimpse the roses.
From the window, the cliffs and cypresses
of San Giminano. On the low table,
a platter with two pomegranates.
One tips its bitten mouth toward us.
The circle of beaten gold around St. Fina
is as round as the gold-scalloped platter,
so now there are three wheels: her halo,
the displayed plate, St. Gregory
in his circle of infants.

Is it this roundness of things
that moves them: wheels, plates, halos,
even the roses which are also like tiny
red mouths in the distance, calling us?
They go round and round like a song,
like a chorus of roundelays,

but the broken pomegranate
bleeds its life
into the larger space.

5. "The Journey of the Three Kings of Oriente"

(a fresco by Benozzo Gozzoli,
Chapel of the Medici-Riccardi Palace)

Round and round like a slow
moving carousel, the pageant
of high and homely citizens moves: servants,
hunters, pilgrims, kings, a bow-
man (a noble headed African), purse-lipped and bald-
pated footmen, clerics. Mild-eyed and curious, some
hunters chase a long-eared Mule deer from
a glorious orchard in the rocks–wild!
Thrilled! The rocks are blue white
and carved like ice, but it's another
season, and calycanthra and pomegranate lend color
to the thousand, ordered, light-
reflecting trees, various, with slim trunks.

The kings are beautiful young boys.
The one in yellow-gold on a white horse
looks dubious, nothing but worldliness
in his young face. His fashionable page
displays a well-turned leg and poses prettily.
Their specialness is in their beauty, followed as they are
by coarser humans: members of the clergy, and far
back, curving out of sight, noblemen and wimpled
ladies, well-dressed on well-dressed horses.
Above them sweeps a swallow, a Florentine bachelor
in coat and tails! A smaller dove's pursued by a comelier
falcon. The deer is outsized, the dove a little clumsy,
inconspicuous, as if Benozzo Gozzoli didn't want his symbols
to overshadow his vivid kinsmen.

What could be more divine than this
well-ordered universe of circling souls,

slowly descending into the gorgeous world,
fruit-laden, a vegetable bliss,
while gold-fleeced clouds canopy their progress?
Right of center, in the uppermost corner,
stands the turreted fortress from which this defection
originated. In the distance a lesser
figure, a straggler caught napping and just now
heard the news, runs after his fellow guests.
They proceed–oblivious, curious, blessed
with fine weather. Their horses illustrate how
horses should canter. The boy kings hold their gifts aloft,
already gifted in their drifting progress.

IV

This Is Missoula

The world is nearly itself
when the black trees hug the snow.
Or in the cool light of the kitchen,
the refrigerator comes on, pumps out
its noisy heart.

And the apples,
blackened and splendid,
knives and spoons
still in their long drawer,
the air like a mirror.

Or mother, at her dark window,
in the broad panels and shadows,
saying, *it's not too late.*
The train draws its slow breath.

Always the bridge between home and town,
the moon in her black well.
This is Missoula. I'll go west
with the first hard snow.
I'll throw my green dress
in the sea.

Leaving Ashland

So we've put on stone shoes in the cruel blue
of evening. Remember in Ashland, the sandstone cliffs
where we reclined in front of the camera? Sun spilled
its careless clouds, the world tinged blue
like milkglass. You were photographing grasses,
agropyron smithii, while I failed another painting.

Where were you going, so intent on the evening?
You kept climbing, framed by the horizon,
as dimly to the north the furious stacks
gave their smoke to the south. I was the one
you had gone beyond choosing–you
with your cargo of solitude.
Soon I'll cut my hair
and wear the loose slacks
I find so comfortable, I'll go
South, lie reading in a garden,
my forehead damp, my wrist tangled
in the hammock. The book is about islands
and the sailors who sliced a bag with a razor
to release the winds, in the beautiful Aegean:
"We are the seed that dies."

The milk has dried in my breast
but there is food from the garden
and the long roses that speak their name,
and the swaying hydrangea.
Soon I will enter the mirror, my hand
at my throat, the apples
dropping in the orchard.

Shiraz

Beyond the hotel grounds the rigid slaves
on pillar after pillar served their king
in stark Persepolis. I taught my sister
how to dance—my beautiful sister—as the band
downstairs began a bossa nova, sending Parisian vocals
over bored, Iranian sands. Too shy
to join the guests, we danced alone
in our hotel room, colliding and dipping
(our two left feet, our drunkenness!).
What were two women doing in Shiraz,
almost thirty, husbandless, afraid
our lives were spinning on without us, while the sky
pulled her starry *chador* across her face
night after night? Poets!
Lovers! Dancers! Where is it written
that beauty is its own reward? So what
if casual roses shed their petals
in brimming waters of the hotel pool
reflecting, as it did, the sequined band,
the air gone palpable as silk pajamas?
Dust funnels hung from heaven on the horizon
like loose threads from a slumming angel's gown.
And so, going forward, nations can
return to centuries of yoke and custom,
as in opening a passage to the future
that winds down through the bowels of Isfahan—
the seven miles of the Bazaar—
to Ali Baba's cave. The rock rolls back.
Back in the States, in malls
lit up with their goods, I'll recall
girlhood dreams of dancing by a pool
where women are admitted into heaven
and history's the fountain we begin from.

American Girl

–for Henri Cole

"Eros at Work"

An intense, orange sun falls into the sea
like Icarus, while an Icarus-like boy
with curved lips and wings waits tables
in this native postcard from the Isle of Lesbos.
Or is he selling her a flower while her lover
sulks at a nearby table, miserable, unshaven?
Poor Eros and his wicked arrows. Always
the instrument, never the object (except for Psyche,
but that's much later). Here he's a lad of sixteen,
working the tables, picking up tips, selling flowers
to a sang-froid beauty. Two celibate loners,
me and my traveling companion,
take the next table. Mid-most
in the middle of our lives, mid-career,
mid-Mediterranean, amid the tourists
and the hustling, handsome waiters,
we write in our diaries: "In Anaxos, always
the sawing lament of the burros.
Is it the sadness of having only two notes
to express, and those rusting
no matter how much you use them? . . ." "Still
constipated." "The wind is delicious,
mild and humid." And later,
back in our separate rooms, we'll dream up
the lovers we wish we'd brought, and no one
will come to mind. "Molivos is famous
for her olives."

To a Friend in the
Hubei Province

You write, "it's a great spot, really—
green, wooded, with rivers flowing . . .
so real, so dreamlike, on the Yangtze River . . ."
Is there a woman with black bangs,
her voice like a cut reed?
Where do you go in the evenings
when your portion of melancholy rises,
the voices almost intelligible,
compliant, the hour approaching
when bells tongue their hollow
vowels and the wheel of the world
rolls over?

In cantinas in Bogotá, in Greek tavernas,
in the East Gate on the sparkling Clark Fork
where wind comes down with a vengeance
through the toothed rocks of the canyon,
someone like you is lifting a glass
to the smoky light, naming
the beautiful ports of the world
in a language so strange, so full of changes
no one can translate it. It speaks through you
of lakes that have fallen from God's eye,
of quartz hills, of doorways through which
women in black dresses carry drinks
of water to men who are drowning,
of places so perfect, so distant,
so fixed in time, no one
can ever leave.

Stars, Fish

Was it your silence that hooked me,
so like a father's? We were fishing
the Blackfoot thirty miles from Ovando.
I always think of us by that river.
Fish sulked in their green house—
the intelligent browns, the beautiful
cutthroat. So deep in the stream
you were *of* the stream, the small bats
brushing your shoulders.

Or was it your past that got to me—
when you worked double shifts
in the zinc mines of Pennsylvania,
stoned on opium, weaving one dream
into another, in the humid blur
of the steam pump? We fished
till the stars came out, till night
filled the woods with smoke.

Now it's as though on the other side
of this life figures move against a screen
in silhouette. You are among them: there,
where there is no language.
You brought that silence back
and burdened me with it. Is it in denial,
then, we find our true voice?

                                    Tonight
I'll name stars: Deneb, Aldebaran, as though
the great North listened, rising up like spruce,
like smoke through the trees and stars
and the great spaces among them
of which we never spoke.

Train to Seattle, Christmas Morning

My Irish friend,
all Winter was against us.
We were held in God's palm
as long as our train rolled
through quarry and depot,
December's tunnel,
and the centuries of snow.

You sang *Barbara Allen*
to the hushed car, in the middle of farmland,
as into the storm's heart, the lull,
our train hurtled. The porter
counted his dollars, blear-eyed, while we retired
to Southern Comfort and ourselves.

Thrumming through the train's
jostle and clockwork,
your highland song: a woman drifting
inside the storm, at home
with feral dogs. I dreamt
of warmer winds, of Howth Head
and the Andalusian girls, the girls
with their tall combs. And the litany
of lines, the *do not send
to ask—love is not love—*
was struck from the track
in the train's speech. I turned my back

on your comfort and music
and faced the glass:
no woman, no wolves, no life
in that snow. Only the deep tone
of the wheel at zero.

A Small Thing

Southeast of Butte the sandstone cliffs turn blue
and light grows visible as ice:
you could step through

and see the world's threads spliced
and weeping, or leave your body and go
wandering, all spirit. Groundsquirrels and mice

dart from their burrows, and low
on the horizon Venus hovers,
too pure for both of us, who know

we'll resume our lives when summer's over.
Our government trailer is well-stocked,
like us, for a future

of accommodation. Thunder lizards rocked
this world once, and over in Rosebud
a tyrannosaurus footprint is locked

in some lucky rancher's outcrop. If we could
fix ourselves at this point: the evening
with its thimbleful of blue, the shifting, hooded

shadows. It's a small thing
to live in a trailer on God's planet,
rocked at night by blasts ripping

open the mines, the generating plant
lit up like an ocean liner
outside our window. What I wanted

was to remain entangled, forever
suspended between one life
and another,

drifting toward morning. The knife
over the bed trembles
and sighs.

Epithalamion

Let the cruel spring begin, Sweeney.
I've had too many lovers as it is,
though I think of them as husbands,
and I think of them,
but it's *me* that I remember.
As if, poised on the brink of a river,
I was part of that river. Take the Mississippi:
nearby in Murphy's Pharmacy
Van Morrison sang *brown-eyed girl*
where Manuel and I wolfed down our hamburgers.
That was Baton Rouge, and, narcissistic,
those songs were always me in my green time.

Not that all this yearn and pull is over.
Far from it: Ophelia's floating
down the Thames in her blue underthings.
Now if my lovers have married other women,
so be it: I don't care. In my best fantasy
I'm beautiful, in a rose-pink gown. It's silly,
yes, I know that–it goes on. I'm surrounded
by animals: sloe-eyed does, pigeons, cows
returned to their wild state–even giraffes–
everyone horned, hoofed, and feathered.

We form one long procession down the levee
among Exxon's refineries, like a page
out of Kipling. You're wondering what's missing
as we move along: no wedding knives,
no altar, and no one in this picture
to declare that beauty.

By Certain Rivers

But what do I remember? Colors. The cottonwood
full of pollen, swollen waters.
These images have hardened into granite
by a tin-colored river. Something about
the agreement of skin and air, sexual,
on the banks of the fathering waters, in fallen
autumn. Father's arrival on *The Constellation*
had us up all night in a waterfront park,
my sisters and I on the swings,
my brothers asleep in the sandbox. Floridian eve,
September had begun its little deaths
among the stinking leaves and sagging woods,
men in dress whites streaming through the park
like the end of the world–*the reckoning*
is coming.

　　　　　　　By certain rivers
women are given over to weeping;
derelicts drink alone or in pairs
to still the beautiful harpies;
by certain rivers
men loading granite onto flatbeds
feel the living resistance of granite;
runaways from the Midwest see their deaths
in the eddying waters, the cottonwood
nodding like horses; by certain rivers
boats are unloading their precious cargo–
cows, sheep, pigs; by certain rivers
we came down and the men surrounded us,
taking us in their arms, their bleached
suits glowing, all the women waving and crying
for those who were coming, those
who were going away.